D1002235

MAE CAROL JEMISON

ASTRONAUT AND EDUCATOR

By Iemima Ploscariu

Content Consultant
Gregory Vogt
Assistant Professor
Center for Educational Outreach
Baylor College of Medicine

Essential Library

An Imprint of Abdo Publishing | abdopublishing.com

ABDOPUBLISHING.COM

Published by Abdo Publishing, a division of ABDO, PO Box 398166, Minneapolis, Minnesota 55439. Copyright © 2018 by Abdo Consulting Group, Inc. International copyrights reserved in all countries. No part of this book may be reproduced in any form without written permission from the publisher. Essential Library™ is a trademark and logo of Abdo Publishing.

Printed in the United States of America, North Mankato, Minnesota
042017
092017

Cover Photo: Bebeto Matthews/AP Images
Interior Photos: Afro American Newspapers/Gado/Archive Photos/Getty Images, 4; JSC/NASA, 6, 9, 10–11, 13, 39, 54, 59, 60, 84; NASA, 11, 25, 56; Paramount/ Everett Collection, 15; AP Images, 16; Jet Lowe/Historic American Buildings Survey/Historic American Engineering Record/Historic American Landscapes Survey/Library of Congress, 19; Jim Cooper/AP Images, 21; Seth Poppel/Yearbook Library, 22, 26, 30, 36; stf/AP Images, 28; iStockphoto, 32, 35, 75; Bob Galbraith/AP Images, 42; Harvey Meston/ Archive Photos/Getty Images, 45; Jonathan Torgovnik/The Hewlett Foundation/Getty Images News/Getty Images, 47; Bettmann/Getty Images, 50; Robert Sullivan/AFP/Getty Images, 63; Time Life Pictures/NASA/The LIFE Picture Collection/Getty Images, 66; Lyndon B. Johnson Space Center/NASA, 67, 69; China Photos/Getty Images News/Getty Images, 72, 80; Lyn Alweis/The Denver Post/Getty Images, 77; MSFC/NASA, 83, 87, 95, 96; Vadim Sadovski/Shutterstock Images, 89; Emilia Ennessy/Shutterstock Images, 91; Marie D. De Jesús/Houston Chronicle/Shutterstock Images, 93

Editor: Susan Bradley
Series Designer: Nikki Farinella

PUBLISHER'S CATALOGING–IN–PUBLICATION DATA

Names: Ploscariu, Iemima, author.
Title: Mae Carol Jemison: astronaut and educator / by Iemima Ploscariu.
Other titles: Astronaut and educator
Description: Minneapolis, MN : Abdo Publishing, 2018. | Series: Women in science | Includes bibliographical references and index.
Identifiers: LCCN 2016962271 | ISBN 9781532110450 (lib. bdg.) | ISBN 9781680788303 (ebook)
Subjects: LCSH: Jemison, Mae,1956- --Juvenile literature. | African American women astronauts--United States--Biography--Juvenile literature. | Women astronauts--United States--Biography--Juvenile literature.
Classification: DDC 629.45/092 [B]--dc23
LC record available at http://lccn.loc.gov/2016962271

CONTENTS

ENDEAVOR TO DREAM

O n the morning of September 12, 1992, Mae Carol Jemison woke up early to prepare for the biggest day of her life. In her room at the Kennedy Space Center in central Florida, she donned a specially designed striped shirt and slacks and then went to breakfast. There, she was joined by the rest of the seven-member crew of the space shuttle *Endeavour:* commander Robert "Hoot" Gibson; pilot Curtis Brown; mission specialists Mark Lee, Dr. Jay Apt, and Dr. Jan Davis; and payload specialist Dr. Mamoru Mohri. They all enjoyed a hearty meal of their choosing, whether the traditional pre-launch breakfast of steak and eggs or something else. The steak-and-eggs meal had become an astronaut tradition ever since Alan Shepard became the first American launched into space in May 1961.

In September 1992, physician Mae Jemison was one of two women on the crew of the space shuttle *Endeavour.*

Jemison savored the meal, hoping she would be able to keep it down once she reached the microgravity environment in space. But the most anticipated part of the breakfast came last: the traditional pre-takeoff cake, complete with the mission's patch made out of frosting.

A UNIQUE MISSION

STS-47, the fiftieth space shuttle flight in National Aeronautics and Space Administration (NASA) history, was characterized by a number of firsts. Jemison was to be the first woman of color in space. Mission specialists Jan Davis and Mark Lee would be the first married couple to fly together, and Dr. Mamoru Mohri would be the first Japanese citizen to travel on a NASA

Jemison, *second from right,* was one of four first-time astronauts on STS-47.

spacecraft. Jemison was also the first astronaut given the title of science mission specialist, meaning she would carry out a variety of life science and materials science experiments on board.

The crew's mission was called Spacelab-J, with the J indicating the mission's major sponsor, Japan's National Space Development Agency (NASDA). The laboratory portion of the shuttle was 23 feet (7 m) long, and it contained the scientific equipment and computers needed to conduct 44 different experiments.[1] Jemison would run experiments that were expected to yield significant findings in medicine and technology.

CLEARED FOR TAKEOFF

After breakfast, the seven astronauts suited up in their orange pressurized suits. Jemison checked her communication headset to ensure a comfortable fit under her helmet. NASA technicians, in turn, scrutinized the crew's suits for any last-minute malfunctions and then deemed them safe for travel. Jemison walked alongside Mohri as they

Mission Patch

Each NASA mission has its own unique patch. The crew members of STS-47 designed theirs to depict the space shuttle with the laboratory module Spacelab-J in its cargo bay. In the background are the flags of the United States and Japan, the two countries that made the mission possible. The land masses of Japan and Alaska are shown, representing the two nations. The initials "SLJ" on the left side stand for the mission's full name: Spacelab Japan. Japanese characters on the right side spell the word for "weightlessness." The crew's last names border the patch.

exited the Operations and Checkout Building. They were taken by bus to the launching pad, smiling and waving to onlookers along the way. Once they entered the *Endeavour*, the astronauts went to their assigned locations, and Jemison strapped herself into her seat on the mid-deck of the shuttle.

US Vice President Dan Quayle was present for the launch, and he sent a message of encouragement to the crew just before takeoff. He asked Captain Gibson to greet Jemison and tell her that students in Detroit, Michigan, at Jemison Academy, which had recently been named in her honor, were watching the launch on television.

Suiting Up

The orange launch entry suit Jemison and the other astronauts wore during launch and reentry was expertly designed but hardly comfortable. It weighed 30 pounds (13.6 kg) and could take up to 30 minutes to put on.[2] Nevertheless, it had features Jemison and the other astronauts needed to keep them safe in an emergency. Made from several layers of breathable material, the suit had tubes of water running through it to regulate the astronauts' temperature. The orange outer layer, which was fireproof, covered an inner layer that could be inflated to maintain the correct air pressure in the event of an emergency. A backup oxygen supply that could last ten minutes was available if needed. The helmet consisted of a hard shell with a face plate that was lowered and sealed during launch and landing. During launch preparations, parachute and survival gear weighing 64 pounds (29 kg) was strapped onto the astronauts once they were seated.[3]

During the space shuttle program, launch entry suits were orange so they would be visible should search and rescue be necessary.

THE SPACE
SHUTTLE

MOBILE LABORATORY

The main components of the space shuttle were the two solid rocket boosters, the external tank, and the orbiter. The two solid rocket boosters provided most of the thrust to lift the shuttle off the launchpad. Three main engines in the orbiter's tail provided additional thrust for liftoff. At an altitude of 28 miles (45 km), the boosters were discarded into the ocean for reuse on another launch.[4] The external tank—the largest part of the shuttle—fueled the orbiter's main engines for the continued journey into space. The tank separated from the orbiter at 70 miles (113 km) from Earth's surface.[5] Finally, two small orbital maneuvering system engines, which flanked the orbiter's tail, completed the push to orbit.

The midsection of the orbiter contained the payload bay where cargo of various kinds, such as the Spacelab, could be mounted. A large, clamshell-like door opened to expose payloads to space. The forward section of the orbiter contained the three-deck crew cabin. Flight controls were located on the upper deck. The lower deck was where astronauts worked and lived. When the Spacelab was on board, a crew transfer tunnel connected the mid-deck to the Spacelab. A collection of small thrusters provided front and rear maneuverability while the shuttle navigated in space. When it came time to return to Earth, the mission commander and pilot flew the orbiter as they would an airplane.

The space shuttle was different from NASA's earliest space vehicles in that the orbiter and solid rocket boosters were reusable on subsequent flights.

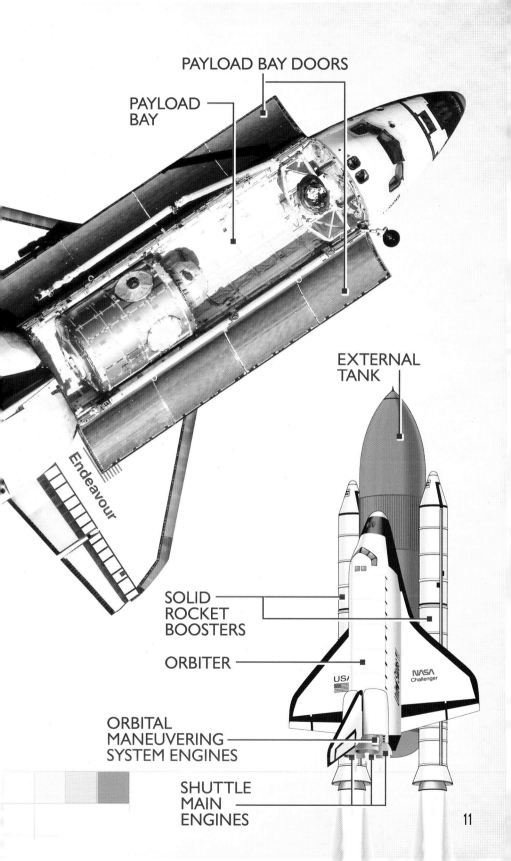

PAYLOAD BAY DOORS

PAYLOAD BAY

Endeavour

EXTERNAL TANK

SOLID ROCKET BOOSTERS

ORBITER

ORBITAL MANEUVERING SYSTEM ENGINES

SHUTTLE MAIN ENGINES

With the space shuttle's systems checked and the crew seated, the operators reported *Endeavour*'s launch configuration was set. The gaseous oxygen vent hood, also known as the beanie cap, was lifted off the external fuel tank. Jemison closed her flight visor as instructed. At 6.6 seconds to launch, the main engines fired. Then the final countdown began. At any moment, they would either be breaking their way through Earth's atmosphere or remembered as heroes of a launch gone wrong. Three, two, one. *Endeavour* successfully launched at 10:23 a.m. Jemison was on her way to explore the cosmos.

When first contacting Mission Control, Jemison led off with the phrase, "All hailing frequencies are

Treasures Aboard

Space shuttle astronauts often brought items aboard that had special meaning or symbolism to them. On her 1992 voyage, Jemison brought a poster from the Alvin Ailey American Dance Theater featuring African-American dancer Judith Jamison in her signature piece, *Cry*. Jemison wanted to reflect her love for dance and her passion for embracing the African-American experience. She also brought a small statue from a women's society in Sierra Leone and a flag from the Organization of African Unity to signify that advances in space travel were for all nations. Other items included a certificate from the Chicago public school system and a banner from Alpha Kappa Alpha, the nation's oldest sorority for black women, both of which symbolized Jemison's dedication to science education. The populations Jemison chose to represent are not usually involved in exploring space. She wanted to show that they possessed the same kind of creativity and potential that made space travel a reality.

Jemison's *Endeavour* voyage was the culmination of her childhood dream to travel into space.

open!"—a phrase she would use to begin all her subsequent radio communications during the flight.[6] This saying is best known for its use by Lieutenant Uhura in the science-fiction television series *Star Trek*.

Jemison had long been a huge *Star Trek* fan. But this was not television. It was reality. And for Jemison, it was the fulfillment of a lifelong dream. She smiled and thought, "If that little girl from Chicago could see her older self now, she would have a huge grin on her face."[7]

TV Cameo

Jemison was a big fan of *Star Trek* ever since watching its inaugural episode in 1966. A few months after her space flight, Jemison was invited to make a guest appearance on a spin-off of the series. In May 1993, she became the first real astronaut to appear on *Star Trek: The Next Generation*, portraying Lieutenant Palmer in the episode "Second Chances."

From her early years in Decatur, Alabama, to adolescence in Chicago, Illinois, and throughout her years of higher education, Jemison longed to visit outer space. But she would go on to make many other contributions in the field of science. Her launch on a sunny morning in 1992 was just the beginning.

Jemison followed in the footsteps of her childhood idol when she appeared in an episode of *Star Trek* in 1993.

14

TWO

GROWING UP

Mae Carol Jemison was born on October 17, 1956, in Decatur, Alabama. Decatur was a city of 30,000 in the northern part of the state, but its close proximity to Huntsville, Alabama, familiarized Decatur residents with NASA early on. Huntsville was home to the Marshall Space Flight Center and the Redstone Arsenal, both of which housed scientists working on rocket-launch technology. Jemison's early exposure to the space industry planted a love of space travel that has stayed with her throughout her life.

FAMILY TIES

Mae's parents, Charlie and Dorothy Jemison, worked hard to provide for their children and encouraged them to be passionate about learning and discovering new things. Charlie was a

From a young age, Mae knew she wanted to be a scientist.

maintenance supervisor, and Dorothy became an elementary school teacher when her children were all enrolled in school. Mae was the youngest of three children, following sister Ada Sue and brother Ricky.

Mae's memories of her time in Decatur mostly involved food. Bee-bops were frozen drinks she and the other children would buy from a neighbor on scorching summer days. Mae demonstrated mechanical aptitude and a desire to try new things at a young age. One day, when her father stepped outside the family car for a moment with the engine running, two-year-old Mae hopped into the front seat, stepped on the clutch, and somehow put the car in gear, making it move. Her success was short-lived, however, as the lurching car dented three nearby vehicles in the process. Mae's brief moment behind the wheel was early evidence of her adventurous and inquisitive spirit.

MOVING NORTH

In 1960, the Jemisons decided to move their family to Chicago, Illinois, so their children would have a chance at a better education. The gains that would be made later by African Americans through the civil rights movement had not yet taken hold in the South, and Dorothy Jemison was discontented with the limited job opportunities available to her in Alabama. She wanted to complete the college education she had discontinued

President Dwight Eisenhower created NASA in 1958. The US Army's Redstone Arsenal in Huntsville, Alabama, became the site of NASA's early rocket research.

to care for her ill parents, and she felt the North was a better place to do that. Mae was three years old when the family left Decatur.

One benefit of the move was that Dorothy was able to start teaching at a Chicago elementary school after completing her college degree. The three Jemison children learned responsibility from an early age, as they usually returned home from school while their parents were still at work.

Mae demonstrated an interest in science at an early age. In 1961, as a kindergartener at McCosh Elementary School in Chicago, she told her teacher she wanted to become a scientist when she grew up. The teacher was so taken aback by Mae's answer that she asked, "Don't you mean a nurse?" At the time, being a nurse was the typical career choice for a girl or young woman interested in science. Mae was offended at the teacher's belief that Mae did not know what a scientist was or that being a scientist was out of reach for her.

In fact, Mae was already on her way to becoming a scientist by discovering how things worked in nature and in the human body. One of her earliest experiments had to do with pus in an infected finger. Fascinated, she ran to her mother, who explained pus was something the body produced to fight

As an adult, Mae still understands the importance of early science education, working as the lead ambassador for the Making Science Make Sense campaign.

germs. Mae's mother encouraged her to read about the topic to learn more.

Mae considered her parents to be the first scientists she knew. They were willing to explore weighty topics at the dinner table, where each family member was expected to have something to contribute to the conversation. Her uncle Louis also encouraged her interest in science and taught her about difficult science concepts, such as physicist Albert Einstein's theory of relativity, when she was only six years old.

As the youngest in the family, Mae had to learn to hold her own. She often joined in when her father invited his male friends over for card games. Interacting with men in such settings helped her develop confidence and not be intimidated later in life, when many of her colleagues were male. As Mae's

A love of dance would follow Mae, *back row center*, to high school and beyond.

confidence grew, her passion and curiosity for studying science only increased each year.

Another activity that captured Mae's imagination was dance. At the age of eight, Mae started ballet lessons at the famous Sadie Bruce Academy in Chicago. She was so determined to dance that, even when her parents could not take her to the studio, she would get there by taking the train. Mae began modern dance lessons a year after starting ballet. Science and dance were formative pillars of Mae's childhood, and she could not imagine one without the other.

FOR THE LOVE OF SCIENCE

Mae's early years in school coincided with the fierce competition

between the United States and the Soviet Union to build a space

program. The Soviet Union took an early lead in the space race,

sending the Sputnik I satellite into orbit in 1957. Then, in 1961,

Soviet cosmonaut Yuri Gagarin became the first human to be

launched into space. Mae, along with much of the nation, took

a keen interest in US space missions. Her third-grade teacher,

Early Space Forays

Mae's early aspirations to travel in space were fueled by watching the Mercury, Gemini, and Apollo space missions. NASA's Project Mercury succeeded in sending the first American astronaut, Alan Shepard, into space in May 1961. Both Shepard and Virgil Grissom, who piloted a flight in July 1961, crewed brief suborbital flights. Suborbital means their velocity was not sufficient to launch them into orbit around Earth. Instead, their spaceships were thrust into space with the aid of rockets, and then they fell back to Earth owing to the pull of gravity. By the third Mercury flight, in 1962, NASA succeeded in launching astronaut

John Glenn into Earth's orbit. Glenn made three passes around Earth in just under five hours, making him an instant national hero. Project Mercury was an important first step for NASA, as scientists learned what it took to send humans into space, how to keep a craft in orbit, and how astronauts were affected by the force of leaving and entering Earth's atmosphere. The Gemini program (1965–1966) tested what happened to astronauts who spent longer periods of time in space. It also let crews practice safely exiting the craft while in space. NASA's crowning achievement came through its Apollo program when, in 1969, it landed the first humans on the moon.

Mrs. Connelly, let the class watch NASA's Gemini launches, and Mae would sometimes run to school so she wouldn't miss them.

Mae had a curious mind, and she was already reading astronomy books in elementary school. She also enjoyed science fiction books such as *A for Andromeda* by Fred Hoyle and John Elliot, *2001: A Space Odyssey* by Arthur C. Clarke, and *I, Robot* by Isaac Asimov. Like many in her generation, she watched every episode of *Star Trek*. Yet, even when reading or watching these fictional stories, Mae asked herself where the women were. She was angry that women scientists were portrayed as heroines in only a few books, such as Madeleine L'Engle's *A Wrinkle in Time* and *The Arm of the Starfish*. It was these few examples, as well as the character of Lieutenant Uhura on *Star Trek*, that sparked her hope and drove her to pursue a career as a scientist.

First Woman in Space

The space race between the United States and the former Soviet Union (USSR) was a significant part of the Cold War (1947–1991) in the 1960s. On June 16, 1963, the USSR launched the first woman into space in the *Vostok 6*. Cosmonaut Valentina Tereshkova made 48 orbits of Earth in three days. In fact, her flight lasted longer than the combined flight time for all the American astronauts up to that date. When Tereshkova made her historic flight, the USSR seemed ahead of the United States in space exploration, but the United States caught up by the end of the decade during NASA's Apollo program.

NASA's second human spaceflight program, Project Gemini, was underway during Mae's elementary school years.

When it was time for Mae to start middle school, a fear of gang violence caused her parents to move the family out of Chicago's Woodlawn neighborhood. They moved into Morgan Park instead, a predominantly white section of Chicago. At Mae's new school, she was able to skip seventh grade and move directly into eighth grade.

THREE

TURBULENCE

Mae approached her teenage years at a time when African Americans were encouraged to stand up for their rights, identify with their black heritage, and not be ashamed of the color of their skin. Although gains made through the civil rights movement made it a hopeful time for African Americans, the lingering effects of discrimination and racial strife were still in force. A major setback in the movement occurred in the spring of 1968, when civil rights leader Martin Luther King Jr. was assassinated in Memphis, Tennessee. The late 1960s were a turbulent time for another reason, too—there were frequent protests against the war in Vietnam. In August 1968, in Mae's hometown of Chicago, violent riots broke out at the Democratic National Convention as war protesters were met

Mae attended an integrated high school in Chicago.

by approximately 12,000 Chicago police officers and 15,000 state and federal troops.[1]

While all this unrest was playing out in the public square, Mae was facing daunting challenges of her own. She was only 12 years old when she entered Morgan Park High School in the fall of 1969. Though she was bright and hardworking, she found it intimidating to enter the high school social scene at her age. Also, although there were many African Americans at her school, the racially charged climate of the time led to some difficult interactions for students. All these factors contributed to Mae later describing her high school years as "tumultuous."[2]

In Mae's first year, she received the worst grade she would earn throughout high school: a D in physical education. She soon learned to follow instructions more carefully and rapidly improved her grade in the class. In addition to academics,

Trouble in the Streets

On August 26, 1968, the Democratic Party convened in Chicago, Illinois, to choose its presidential candidate for the coming election. The party was sharply divided on the issue of the Vietnam War. Outside the convention hall, antiwar protesters clashed with police. Riots broke out, and Mayor Richard Daley called in nearly 12,000 police officers, who were aided by 7,500 national guardsmen and 7,500 US Army soldiers.[3] Violence escalated as police beat and gassed demonstrators, journalists, and even doctors. In all, 119 police officers and 100 protesters were injured.[4] Mae witnessed the battle between protesters and police and was frightened by the authorities' show of force.

Mae witnessed the violent clashes between police and antiwar protesters at the 1968 Democratic National Convention in Chicago.

Mae with the student council during her senior year

she was involved in many extracurricular activities. She was a cheerleader and president of the student council, president of the Modern Dance Club, and president of the Russian Club, as well as an honor-roll student. One of Mae's high school highlights was getting to dance in her favorite musical, *West Side Story*. She found that dancing trained her to practice good habits, sharpened her memory, strengthened her physically, and gave her coordination. Mae's passion for dance in high school was matched only by her love of science.

STUDYING SICKLE CELLS

Mae was always looking for new science experiments to conduct and new topics to study. In her junior year of high school, Mae's mother suggested she do her science fair project on sickle cell anemia. Mae learned sickle cell anemia is a genetic blood disease that is most common in people of African origin. It receives its name from the hooked shape of the red blood cells in people afflicted with the condition. Unlike normal, round blood cells, sickle cells are shaped like crescent moons, which makes them ineffective carriers of oxygen through the bloodstream.

Wanting to learn more but not knowing how to begin her research, Mae mustered up the courage to call Cook County Hospital and ask for the chief hematology lab technician, who studies blood diseases. After a brief talk, he invited her to intern at the hospital while she conducted research for her project. Twice a week

Desegregation

In 1954, the US Supreme Court case *Brown v. Board of Education* determined racial segregation in public schools violated the equal protection clause of the Fourteenth Amendment. Although *Brown* did not have the effect of fully desegregating public schools, it put the full weight of the federal government behind desegregation efforts. Morgan Park High School, which Mae attended, was an integrated school from its founding in 1916. In contrast, many of Chicago's high schools became heavily segregated in the 1960s as white families moved from the city to the surrounding suburbs.

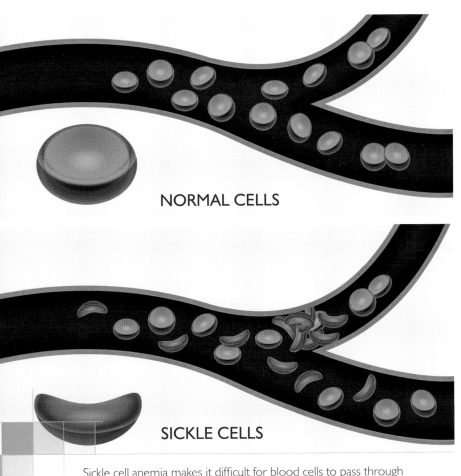

NORMAL CELLS

SICKLE CELLS

Sickle cell anemia makes it difficult for blood cells to pass through blood vessels.

for one month, she traveled to the hospital's hematology lab on Chicago's West Side.

The technician showed her how to diagnose sickle cell anemia and how to identify the blood patterns of a person who had sickle cell anemia, or even just the sickle cell trait. A person with only the trait is a carrier of the disease but experiences no symptoms. He also showed her what normal blood cells looked like under the microscope compared to sickle cells. The technician and other staff members in the hematology department were impressed with how quickly Mae learned. In fact, the head of the department treated Mae like a colleague, assigned her to read scientific papers, and challenged her to test a compound to see if it would make sickle cells revert to normal cells. Mae chose a compound, tested it, observed what effect it had on the sickle cells, and wrote a scientific paper on the experiment. In addition to earning her a good grade on her school project and a first-place finish in the citywide science fair, the experience fostered an interest in biochemistry that would shape her future career.

Morning Math

In her last year of high school, Mae's math teacher, David Drymiller, recognized her aptitude for math and science. He and Mae discussed ways in which he could provide her with more challenging math to prepare her for engineering courses in college. Mae, her friend Sheila, and Drymiller agreed to meet every weekday morning at seven so he could teach them solid analytical geometry and calculus. Solid analytical geometry is the study of geometric objects in three-dimensional space. Calculus provides a means of deducing how variables such as speed and acceleration change over time. Mae studied these subjects on top of being enrolled in Algebra III and trigonometry. She also took summer-school science classes throughout high school to be exposed to as much science as possible.

Another of Mae's academic interests involved engineering. The Junior Engineering Technical Society sponsored a program at the University of Illinois at Urbana-Champaign the summer before Mae's senior year to increase students' awareness of various engineering specialties. After the two-week program, Mae was enthralled with the new field of biomedical engineering. As she later commented, "I was able to reconcile my love of physics, biology, practical implementation, and creativity in this one area of biomedical engineering."[5] The program opened new avenues of exploration for Mae and spurred her on to pursue a career as a scientist.

In 1973, at just 16 years old, Mae graduated from Morgan Park High School. She was awarded a National Achievement Scholarship and received college acceptance offers from prestigious schools such as the Massachusetts Institute of Technology and Stanford University. After careful deliberation, taking into account both academic and social pros and cons, Mae chose Stanford and prepared herself to move west to California. For the first time in her life, the Chicago train system wasn't able to take her where she needed to go.

SCIENCE
SPOTLIGHT

SICKLE CELL DISEASE

Sickle cell disease (SCD) is an umbrella term for a group of inherited red blood cell disorders. People with SCD have abnormal hemoglobin—the protein that carries oxygen throughout the body—in their red blood cells. Normal red blood cells are disc-shaped and flexible, enabling them to move through even the smallest blood vessels to deliver oxygen. A person with sickle cell anemia has red blood cells that are stiff and curved, preventing their smooth passage through vessels and thus diminishing the transport of oxygen to tissues. These cells can stick to vessel walls, completely blocking the flow of blood. This oxygen shortage results in both acute and chronic pain, as well as long-term organ damage. Another characteristic of sickle cells is inflexibility, which causes them to burst after a short time. Normal red blood cells can live as long as 120 days, but sickle cells last no more than ten to 20 days. This rapid die-off means the body has a difficult time keeping up its production levels of red blood cells, so anemia results. The only cure for sickle cell disease is a specialized form of stem-cell transplant, but few sufferers of SCD are able to find an appropriate donor match. Other treatments can help manage symptoms and prolong life, but early diagnosis and regular medical care are essential.

FOUR

CAREER DILEMMAS

In the fall of 1973, Jemison entered Stanford University as a freshman intending to study biomedical engineering. Stanford's strong engineering and medical programs were not the only reason Mae decided to enroll there; she also loved that Stanford had a good football team and that the San Francisco Bay Area was known for innovation in the arts and sciences.

STANFORD RIGORS

Upon arrival, Jemison was picked up from the San Francisco airport by a representative of the Stanford Black Student Union. They drove onto campus through the famous Palm Drive with tall, sentry-like palm trees seeming to herald her arrival. She was assigned to Alondra House within Florence Moore Hall, a coed dorm that housed all levels of students, from freshmen to

Jemison enjoyed both academic and extracurricular activities at Stanford.

seniors. None of the dorm residents seemed to think any less of her because of her young age. Jemison, a true football lover, enjoyed the chance to play football for the first time on the dorm's intramural team.

Engineering Fields

Jemison majored in chemical engineering, but much of her later work encompassed biomedical engineering. Though the two occasionally overlap, they rely on different principles of science. Biomedical engineers bridge medicine and engineering to improve health care. They design and create devices such as automated monitoring machines used on surgical patients, astronauts, and deep-sea divers. They also develop devices to replace damaged or missing body parts, such as hearing aids, pacemakers, artificial kidneys and hearts, synthetic blood vessels, and prosthetic limbs. Laser eye surgery, heart catheters, ultrasounds, and magnetic resonance imaging are all the result of biomedical research. Chemical engineers, by contrast, primarily use the principles of chemistry (along with biology and physics) to design equipment for pharmaceutical companies and other manufacturing companies. They develop ways to make medicine more affordable, improve food processing techniques, and create safer ways to refine petroleum. Jemison's experience in both fields made her a well-rounded engineer.

Originally, Jemison intended to continue studying Russian, since she felt it would be useful as she pursued a career in space exploration. However, Jemison's first engineering academic adviser was not supportive regarding her language studies. He also suggested she take freshman engineering courses, disregarding the superior preparation she had received in high school. Though discouraged about the suggestion to drop Russian, Jemison heeded his advice and picked up Swahili instead, but she also sought

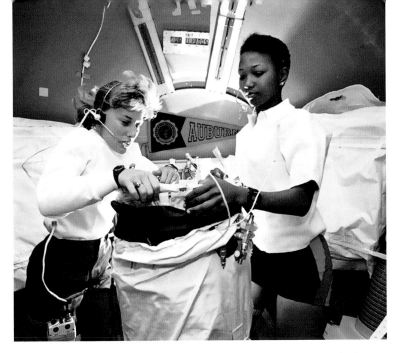

Jemison's wide background in engineering would aid her later during her career as an astronaut.

out a different adviser. Her second adviser, who was also an engineering professor, encouraged Jemison to get a degree in chemical engineering since Stanford's biomedical engineering program was still being developed.

The summer after her freshman year, Jemison worked for Bell Labs in Illinois, broadening her education to include computer programming. Throughout her undergraduate studies, Jemison often enrolled in difficult graduate-level courses when the subject matter appealed to her, including classes on life science, space exploration, and biomedical fluid mechanics. The latter involves using engineering principles to study how blood and other fluids flow in the body. Jemison's studies

African-American Heritage

The novel *Roots*, by Alex Haley, was published in 1976 when Jemison was a junior in college. The book is about an African man named Kunta Kinte. Captured as a teenager in the 1700s, he is sold into slavery in the United States. The story follows the life of Kinte's descendants down through the centuries to Haley. *Roots* was a *New York Times* best seller for 46 weeks, and it was made into a television miniseries in 1977. *Roots* provoked important discussions about race in American society and reflected the growing interest among African Americans in learning about their heritage. In 2006, Harvard University professor Henry Louis Gates Jr., who had been inspired by Haley's work, invited Jemison to be one of eight African Americans profiled in his video series, *African American Lives*. Gates used historical documents to trace the subjects' family trees and then enlisted leading geneticists to conduct DNA analyses. Jemison learned her ancestors had been enslaved in Talladega County, Alabama.

also extended to advanced topics such as partial differential equations and heat-transfer theory.

NOT ONLY A SCIENTIST

In the early 1970s, the black empowerment movement began taking shape—especially in California, where groups such as the Black Panthers had recently formed. Jemison took all the African-American literature, history, and African studies classes her science-heavy schedule allowed. As a student, she designed and helped teach two classes: Race and Politics in Education and Race and Culture in the Caribbean. She also pursued her love of dance, performing in African and modern dance groups and choreographing dance pieces. Jemison landed roles in the university production of the Pulitzer Prize–winning play *No Place to Be Somebody* and in the musical comedy *Purlie*. During her senior year, she also became involved in student politics, serving as president of the Black Student Union.

Jemison's passion for the arts and sciences and for her African-American heritage led her to pursue the equivalent of a double major in chemical engineering and Afro-American studies. During her Stanford career, Jemison encountered a few professors who marginalized her or were prejudiced against her on the basis of her young age, gender, or race, but she took those difficult situations as opportunities to strengthen her character. For the most part, she described her years at Stanford as "wonderful and very positive."[1]

As her 1977 graduation approached, Jemison was trying to decide between pursuing a dancing career and going to medical school. As usual, she asked her mother for advice. Dorothy Jemison replied, "You can always dance if you're a doctor, but you can't doctor if you're a dancer."[2] So, Jemison enrolled at Cornell University Medical College in New York City. Before moving to New York, Jemison spent the summer working in San Jose, California, as an engineer for IBM.

CHAPTER FIVE

DANCING DOCTOR

J emison arrived in New York City in the fall of 1977. She was 20 years old, tall, slender, and she wore two earrings in one ear and a feather in the other. She did not fit the stereotype of a medical student at Cornell University Medical College, yet she was confident in who she was as a person and a student. Her years at Stanford had prepared her academically and had stretched her as a young woman setting out on her own.

CULTURE SHOCK

At Olin Hall, the dormitory for medical students, Jemison met fellow first-year students Joan Culpepper and Blaine Morton. Jemison and Culpepper were roommates, and they, plus Morton, became good friends and study partners. During her first evening at Cornell, Jemison impressed several of the older

In the next decade, Jemison's characteristic confidence would see her through medical school, medical missions to Africa, and ultimately becoming an astronaut.

medical students with her skill at playing whist, one of her favorite card games.

Jemison's first class at Cornell was Gross Anatomy, which required her to dissect a human cadaver. Her initial reaction was shock and disgust at having to touch a dead body. After a difficult few weeks, she overcame her aversion and appreciated the opportunity to see firsthand what blood vessels, nerves, organs, and bones looked like and where they were located in the body. Jemison was overwhelmed with the demanding workload her first semester. She studied long hours each day and stayed up late at night to memorize class material. Many of her classmates had pursued premedical majors in college and were more familiar with the subject matter. To get tips on how to avoid falling behind, she called her sister, Ada Sue, who was in her fourth year at Washington University School of Medicine in Saint Louis, Missouri. Ada Sue sent some books for Jemison to review, and Jemison also joined a biochemistry study group. Once the medical concepts became more familiar to her, she found time for the extracurricular activities she loved.

SETTLING IN

Whenever Jemison had some extra money, she spent it on modern and African dance classes at the Alvin Ailey American Dance Theater, a place she had long dreamed of visiting. Dancing provided an outlet for her energy and helped her

Although Stanford prepared her well for a career in chemical engineering, Jemison was challenged in her early classes at Cornell University Medical College.

relieve tension from the many hours spent studying. Jemison also became involved in student politics, as she had been at Stanford. She took her first international trip in the summer of 1978 to do research in Cuba and help at a Cambodian refugee camp in Thailand.

In her second year of medical school, Jemison bought her first medical instruments and learned how to do a physical diagnosis, practicing first on other students and then on patients. She aimed to put into practice what her instructors taught: be precise, be thorough, and treat patients with respect. In the spring of 1979, Jemison organized a citywide health and law fair in New York City, where, as president, she represented the Cornell chapter of the Student National Medical Association.

Dance Legacy

The Alvin Ailey American Dance Theater made its New York City debut on March 30, 1958. The troupe of young, black dancers was and still is recognized for its creativity and boldness in American dance culture. From an early age, Jemison was drawn to its work and was an ardent fan of Ailey's most beloved dancer, Judith Jamison. Jemison lived out the Ailey legacy: "To use dance as a medium for honoring the past, celebrating the present, and fearlessly reaching into the future."[1]

AFRICAN TRAVELS

During the summer of 1979, Jemison went to Kenya to work with the African Medical and Research Foundation (AMREF). She joined with doctors from various developed countries to provide health

AMREF is one of many organizations working to improve health care in Kenya and the rest of Africa.

AMREF

The African Medical and Research Foundation (AMREF) is the largest African-based nonprofit organization delivering health services. It was founded in 1957 by physicians Thomas Rees, Michael Wood, and Archibald McIndoe as the Flying Doctors of East Africa. Initially, the three doctors flew on small planes to deliver medical care and emergency medical supplies to isolated communities in Africa. Today, the organization is headquartered in Nairobi, Kenya, and has staff in more than 30 countries. AMREF trains and supports African health workers to improve access to quality care in local communities. Staff members also address key health issues such as sanitation and access to clean water. With more than 160 programs and offices in Ethiopia, Senegal, South Africa, South Sudan, Tanzania, and Uganda, AMREF's vision is to see lasting health-care improvements in Africa.

care in remote parts of East Africa. Jemison conducted a survey of the local population's health in the Embu district of Kenya. Her data collection included visiting villagers' homes and documenting their vaccination statuses and the height and weight of any children in the homes. Jemison also assisted with surgeries at a hospital in the town of Voi and saw a baby being delivered. She was thrilled to be in Africa after studying the continent's history, culture, and politics. Jemison took the opportunity of being overseas to explore North Africa and Israel before beginning her third year of medical school.

Jemison survived the difficult clinical rotations in her third year, learning from and assisting a series of doctors with specific specialties, such as pediatrics or surgery. Then she successfully completed her last year of medical studies. In 1981, she graduated from Cornell University Medical College, ready to move on to a one-year residency program and become a licensed physician. But Jemison's goals included more than a traditional medical career. Her main reason for having gone to medical school in the first place was to pursue a career in biomedical engineering research, but in the meantime, she longed to return to a developing country to deliver much-needed primary care. At the same time, Jemison never lost sight of the career goal she set for herself as a young girl: to travel in space.

Speaking Swahili

Jemison's Swahili-language studies at Stanford helped her communicate with the local African health workers when she worked in Kenya. Swahili is the second-most common language in Africa. It originated from the Bantu culture, but like most languages, it has other linguistic influences as well, including Arabic. Swahili is used primarily in East and Central Africa. The traditional speakers of the language call it Kiswahili.

A HEART
FOR AFRICA

After finishing at Cornell, Jemison fulfilled a one-year internship at the Los Angeles County–University of Southern California Medical Center. During her year in Los Angeles, she trained in pediatrics, treated infectious diseases, assisted with surgery, administered cancer treatments, and worked in the emergency room. Her internship required hands-on work that put into practice what she had learned in medical school.

Throughout her internship, Jemison explored different options for going overseas again. She was willing to work as either a doctor or an engineer, as her primary goal was to make a positive difference in a less developed country.

As a new physician, Jemison interned in Los Angeles to start her medical career.

CORPS DECISIONS

In 1983, Jemison applied for and was accepted as Area Peace Corps Medical Officer for Sierra Leone and Liberia. She would be the physician for Peace Corps volunteers and US embassy staff serving in West Africa. Her responsibilities included supervising the rest of the medical staff and managing the laboratory, medical office, and pharmacy. She also trained all incoming volunteers on how to care for their own health while in Africa. Jemison was on call 24 hours a day, seven days a week, and she had to be prepared to handle medical emergencies at a moment's notice.

A particularly frightening situation happened just two weeks after her arrival. One of the Peace Corps volunteers in Sierra Leone became sick, and a staff doctor diagnosed the illness as malaria. Jemison administered chloroquine, the standard treatment for malaria, but the patient's symptoms worsened.

JFK's Legacy

The Peace Corps, an independent agency within the US government, sends volunteers to developing countries to lend medical, technical, and educational aid. Senator John F. Kennedy proposed the idea of the Peace Corps in 1960 while speaking to 10,000 students at the University of Michigan. Once he became president, Kennedy signed an executive order that made the Peace Corps a reality on March 1, 1961. More than 220,000 Americans have served in the Peace Corps in countries throughout the world to create better understanding and collaboration among nations and cultures.[1]

Jemison was sure he had meningitis instead. Then, at two o'clock in the morning, the hospital's electricity went out. Jemison used a flashlight to locate the necessary antibiotics.

As they monitored the patient's condition, Jemison and the staff realized they lacked the medicine and medical supplies needed to fight the infection. Jemison, only 26 years old at the time and brand new to her job, ordered a medical evacuation of the patient to Germany. The US embassy staff was reluctant to carry out this $80,000 order, as they considered it to be hasty and unnecessary, but Jemison firmly explained she was the medical officer in charge of saving this volunteer's life, and she intended to do so.[2]

Jemison accompanied the patient to the Air Force hospital in Germany, where doctors successfully treated his meningitis. After 56 hours

Freshwater Dangers

While in Africa, Jemison researched and trained others to treat schistosomiasis, the second-most devastating parasitic disease, after malaria. More than 200 million people are infected with schistosomiasis worldwide.[3] Also known as bilharzia, schistosomiasis is caused by parasitic worms that live in certain types of freshwater snails. These worms are found in tropical and subtropical regions, with the vast majority of their impact occurring in Africa. People can become infected when their skin comes into contact with water in which the parasites reside. The worms penetrate human skin and lay eggs, which travel to the intestine, liver, or bladder of the infected person. Most people do not experience the common symptoms of itchy skin, coughing, fever, or muscle aches until one to two months after infection first occurs. Over a period of time the eggs can cause inflammation, scarring, and damage to internal organs. Schistosomiasis can be effectively treated with the drug praziquantel, which kills adult worms with a single dose.

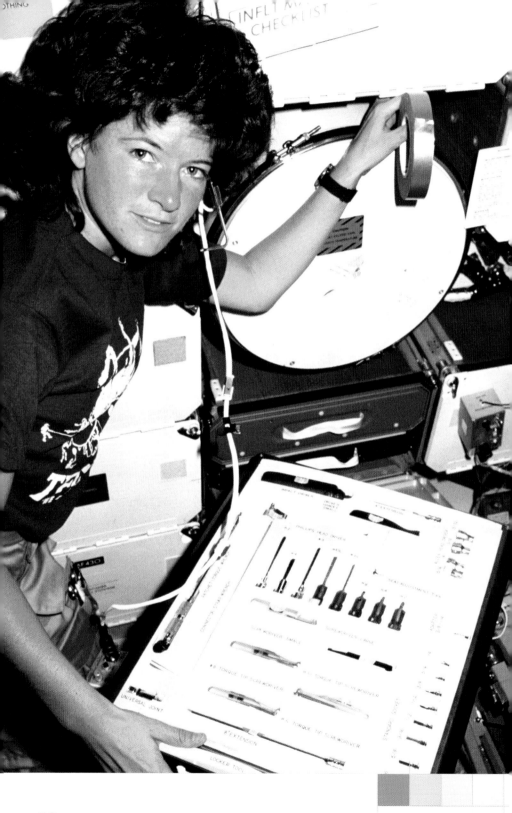

without sleep, Jemison could finally rest, but she was soon on her way back to Sierra Leone to continue her job.

During her time in West Africa, Jemison led a research project funded by the National Institutes of Health and the Centers for Disease Control. Her research concerned infectious diseases such as hepatitis B, schistosomiasis, and rabies. She also wrote guides for Peace Corps volunteers about public health and safety guidelines in Africa, as well as booklets for local Africans on how they could best take care of their health. Jemison's efforts helped save and improve the lives of many people during her two years in the Peace Corps.

While Jemison was working in West Africa, two historic events took place in the US space program. In June 1983, Sally Ride became the first American woman to go into space, and in August of that year, Guion "Guy" Bluford became the first African American to do so. Ride's and Bluford's

Sally's Ride

On June 18, 1983, Sally Ride became the first American woman to go into space, making her only the third woman on the planet to do so. Ride was a mission specialist and flight engineer onboard the *Challenger* STS-7. She spent six days in space working a robotic arm that helped place satellites in orbit. A year later, she was part of the crew on a second mission. Born in Los Angeles, Ride chose a career in physics over becoming a professional tennis player. Like Jemison, she graduated from Stanford University. Ride's flight inspired many to recognize the potential of women in mostly male careers. Following her time at NASA, Ride became the director of the California Space Institute at the University of California, San Diego. She died of cancer in 2012.

In 1983, physicist Sally Ride was the third woman to go into space, following two Russian cosmonauts in 1963 and 1982.

example, as well as NASA's demonstrated openness to diversity, encouraged Jemison to hold on to her dream of space travel.

BACK TO LA

After her years as a Peace Corps medical officer, Jemison returned to Los Angeles, where she began work as a primary care physician. At the same time, she continued to pursue her dreams related to biomedical engineering and space exploration. She took night courses in engineering at the University of California, Los Angeles, and in 1985 applied to be an astronaut with NASA. As she waited for a reply, a tragic event occurred. In January 1986, the space shuttle *Challenger* exploded during its climb to orbit, and the entire crew was killed. NASA grounded the space shuttle program while it investigated the disaster and implemented safety changes. Jemison refused to give up her dream of space travel. When the program reopened, she applied again.

Breaking the Color Barrier

Guion "Guy" Bluford was a colonel in the US Air Force and a veteran of the Vietnam War (1954–1975). On August 30, 1983, Bluford was a mission specialist on the shuttle *Challenger* for mission STS-8, which required the deployment of a satellite into orbit. STS-8 came back to Earth after six days in space. Bluford broke NASA's color barrier by becoming the first African American to travel into space, opening the door to Jemison and many others. Bluford flew three more missions for a total of 28 days in space. His career after NASA has included leadership positions in several engineering companies.

Prior to becoming an astronaut, Guy Bluford studied aerospace engineering and was a fighter pilot in the US Air Force, earning the rank of colonel.

In January 1987, she received a thick envelope from NASA in the mail. NASA wanted to interview her at Johnson Space Center in Houston, Texas. Jemison was one of 100 interviewees chosen from among the 2,000 qualified applicants. Finally, after a lengthy interview process, she received a call in June welcoming her as one of 15 new astronauts-in-training. Jemison quit her job in Los Angeles, packed up her cat, Sneeze, and moved to Houston.

A Nation Mourns

On January 28, 1986, the seven-member crew of NASA mission STS-51L boarded the space shuttle *Challenger*. The crew consisted of spacecraft commander Dick Scobee, pilot Michael Smith, mission specialists Judith Resnik, Ronald McNair, and Ellison Onizuka, payload specialist Gregory Jarvis, and high school social studies teacher Christa McAuliffe. McAuliffe was selected as the first teacher in the NASA "Teacher in Space" program. NASA hoped having McAuliffe teach lessons from space and broadcasting them to schools around the country would create more public interest in the space program.

The launch at Kennedy Space Center in central Florida was delayed a number of times because of bad weather. NASA finally decided to blast off at 11:40 a.m. Seventy-three seconds after liftoff, a huge fireball could be seen in the sky. All seven crew members died, most likely when their cabin hit the ocean surface at more than 200 miles per hour (322 kmh).[4] Later analysis determined a leak in one of the solid rocket booster joints had caused blowtorch-like flames to burn through and ignite the main fuel tank. The explosion, witnessed by millions of Americans via television rebroadcasts, was devastating to the American public and led NASA to ground its space shuttle program for nearly three years.

The space shuttle *Challenger* successfully completed nine NASA missions prior to its catastrophic launch in January 1986.

SEVEN

THE NASA YEARS

J emison arrived at her new home in Houston in June 1987 to join NASA's newest group of astronauts-in-training at Johnson Space Center. The nation was still recovering from the tragic loss of the *Challenger* crew, and many people inside and outside the space program were doubtful as to what lay ahead for NASA. Jemison was one of two women, along with Jan Davis, in the class of 15 astronauts, the majority of whom already worked for NASA or were part of the military.

LEARNING CURVE

The candidates represented a wide range of sciences, including mechanical engineering, medicine, meteorology, and astrophysics. The group also included test pilots and a NASA flight controller. They learned to apply their field of

Jemison examines the laboratory module of Spacelab-J during her extensive training for the STS-47 mission.

expertise to space travel but were also taught a wide range of new information. Jemison learned how a spacecraft functions differently from the airplanes they used for training. She analyzed the causes of the *Challenger* disaster and memorized the inner workings of the space shuttle. She studied the physics behind orbiting Earth and how the body reacts to microgravity. Course content included, among other subjects, planetary characteristics, geology, and meteorology.

Along with math and science classes, the astronauts went through difficult physical preparation. They received parachute and survival training to prepare them for flying in the T-38 supersonic jet, which offered practice functioning in high-stress environments. Since Jemison was classified as a mission specialist, she did not have to learn to fly the planes on her own, but she was trained to manage the radios and controls, keep the plane on course once it left the ground, and be ready to assist the pilot in an emergency. The crew also took training flights on the KC-135, a reduced-gravity aircraft that afforded a near-weightless experience.

Vomit Comet

The KC-135 was the infamous training aircraft known as the Vomit Comet. Two of every three fliers who trained on it became sick when the plane did its U-shaped maneuvers over the Gulf of Mexico. The parabolic pattern of flight created a free-fall feeling much like riding up and down a steep roller coaster. Trainees experienced approximately 20 seconds of microgravity.

Jemison climbing out of the T-38 training jet, September 1992

NASA provided simulators at Johnson Space Center's Space Vehicle Mockup Facility to prepare the astronauts for microgravity while in orbit. Jemison and the others practiced again and again with these systems. They practiced stowing away their suits, flying the shuttle, and taking simulated space walks in the underwater Weightless Environment Training Facility. On the Precision Air-Bearing Floor, the astronauts were taught to move large objects as they would in space, where there is no friction to resist movement. The floor resembled a life-size air hockey game. Although NASA could not exactly replicate space conditions, the seasoned trainers prepared Jemison and her colleagues well.

WAITING GAME

Jemison completed her year of training in 1988 and was qualified to be a mission specialist on space shuttle flights, but she had to wait several years before being assigned to a mission. In the meantime, Jemison tested software on shuttles at Johnson Space Center and served as a technical liaison between the Johnson and Kennedy Space Centers.

Later that year, Jemison went to Florida to help with the launch of STS-26, the first space shuttle mission after the *Challenger* explosion. Jemison heard on the radio that Nichelle Nichols, the actress who portrayed Lieutenant Uhura on *Star Trek*, was in Orlando at a convention. Nichols and her company,

The Space Shuttle

From 1981 to 2011, NASA's space shuttle program launched more than 350 people on 135 missions in five different shuttles. The five shuttles included *Columbia*, the first to launch on April 12, 1981, along with *Challenger*, *Discovery*, *Atlantis*, and *Endeavour*. The shuttles received their names from noteworthy oceangoing ships in history. Jemison's shuttle, *Endeavour*, was named after the first ship of eighteenth-century explorer Captain James Cook. In addition to the *Challenger* disaster in 1986, another tragic loss occurred in 2003 when *Columbia* disintegrated upon reentry, claiming the lives of all seven astronauts aboard. NASA engineers were aware that a piece of foam weighing less than two pounds (0.9 kg) had broken off from the external tank during liftoff. They believe the foam struck and damaged the left wing and made the shuttle more vulnerable to the extreme heat experienced during reentry. Despite the many advances made through the shuttles' cutting-edge research, funding constraints resulted in the demise of the program. *Atlantis* carried the last mission back to Earth on July 21, 2011, marking the end of an era. The surviving orbiters, *Discovery*, *Atlantis*, and *Endeavour*, can be found at museums in Virginia, Florida, and California, respectively.

Women in Motion, were instrumental in getting people of color to apply to NASA when the astronaut program was seeking to hire women and members of racial minorities in the mid-1970s. Jemison decided to take advantage of the opportunity and went to the convention to meet Nichols. She was surprised to find Nichols was as excited to meet her as she was to meet Nichols. Their meeting was the start of an enduring friendship as well as many years of professional collaboration.

Finally, in August 1989, the long-awaited news arrived. Jemison received her assignment as a science mission specialist for STS-47, Spacelab-J, on the space shuttle *Endeavour*. Since Spacelab-J was sponsored by the Japanese government's space agency, NASDA, and 35 of the 44 experiments were designed by Japanese scientists, Jemison went with future crew members Jan Davis and Mark Lee to Japan to be trained on how to run the projects. They worked with future crew member Mamoru Mohri and spent a total of two years training in both the United States and Japan. The mission gave Jemison the opportunity to experience another culture and help two nations collaborate in the promotion of science.

WORKING IN SPACE

After nearly six years of training, Jemison's launch day finally arrived. Jemison and the crew of STS-47 *Endeavour* blasted

Americans Jemison, Davis, and Lee trained in Japan with crewmate Mamoru Mohri (*second from left*), a fluid physicist who was an expert in vacuum and materials sciences.

The *Endeavour* crew, experiencing microgravity on their first day in space, pose for the traditional in-flight portrait.

into orbit on September 12, 1992. Once they left Earth's atmosphere, the crew members took off their orange pressurized suits and began performing their assigned tasks. Jemison was on the mid-deck putting away the suits when Captain Gibson called her up to the flight deck. There, through the ship's window, the first thing she saw from space was her hometown of Chicago. Her childhood dream of making it to

Frog Embryology

While on her space flight, Jemison examined frogs to see if gravity was needed for an amphibian egg to be fertilized and reach the tadpole stage. Adult female frogs were taken aboard *Endeavour* to shed their eggs. Half of the fertilized eggs were fixed, or stopped from developing, so they could be studied back on Earth. The other half were permitted to develop in microgravity. The results showed gravity is not necessary for successful reproduction; vertebrates can fertilize and develop normally in microgravity.

outer space had come true. But now, what Jemison called the "real work" of turning the shuttle into a laboratory was yet to be done.[1]

Jemison was part of the Blue Shift team with Jan Davis and Jay Apt. Every 12 hours, the Blue team passed control of the orbiter functions and the space lab to the Red Shift team. This way, half of the crew was manning the shuttle and conducting experiments around the clock. Of the 44 experiments, 24 concerned materials science and 20 were related to life science. The materials science experiments tested different electronic, glass, ceramic, metal, and alloy materials for their suitability in semiconductors, which are used in making computer chips. The life science experiments included measuring the cell life of different organisms, testing how humans and several animal species react to changes in atmospheric pressure, and creating a fluid therapy system to see if intravenous fluids could be successfully produced and administered in space in an emergency. Frog fertilization and biofeedback treatment for motion sickness in space were also among the important studies conducted. Jemison was particularly interested in the lower body negative-pressure tests. As one of the test subjects, Jemison stood in a waist-high tube with an airtight seal around her waist. A pump then sucked the air out of the tube for 50 minutes to create negative pressure around her legs, pulling blood from her upper body. The test, which recorded pulse rate, blood pressure, and cardiac function, measured how her heart adjusted to the change in pressure. The purpose of this

Jemison and Jan Davis conduct a lower body negative-pressure test to simulate gravity. The test measures cardiovascular responses to stress.

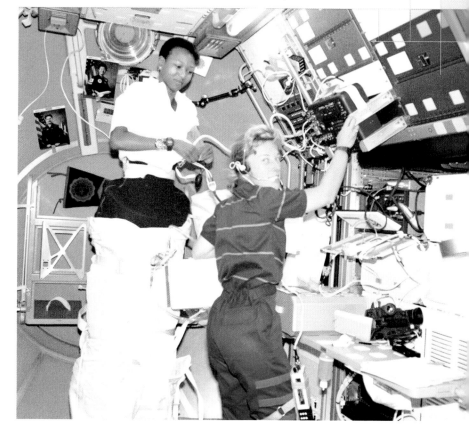

Earth-to-Space Radio

One of the experiments conducted on the mid-deck of STS-47 was the Shuttle Amateur Radio Experiment (SAREX). The purpose of SAREX was to test the feasibility of the shuttle crew being in contact with amateur radio operators on the ground. In addition, SAREX provided an opportunity for schools all over the world to connect with the *Endeavour* in space. SAREX was an exciting educational tool for students, as they were able to speak directly to Jemison and the other astronauts as they orbited the planet.

experiment was to find ways to help astronauts readjust when they returned to Earth.

After almost eight days and 126 orbital revolutions, the space shuttle *Endeavour* returned to Earth with its crew on September 20, 1992. Jemison spent seven days, 22 hours, 30 minutes, and 23 seconds in space, traveling a distance of 3,271,844 miles (5,265,523 km).[2] At 8:53 a.m., the shuttle landed at Kennedy Space Center's Runway 33, and Captain Gibson informed the NASA personnel monitoring the flight from Houston that they had come to a complete stop. Houston's response: "Roger wheel stop, *Endeavour*. Congratulations on a highly successful and historic mission."[3] Breaking multiple barriers, Jemison had become the first female African-American astronaut to experience space travel.

SCIENCE
SPOTLIGHT

BIOFEEDBACK

The microgravity environment in space typically causes unpleasant effects on astronauts for the first few days of flight. Common symptoms include headaches, backaches, nausea, loss of appetite, and confusion as the astronauts tumble through the shuttle. Medication is available to treat the motion sickness, but unpleasant side effects can hinder crew members from completing their work. NASA researcher and psychologist Patricia Cowings encouraged the use of biofeedback during space shuttle flights as a remedy. Biofeedback is a technique that was first used in clinical practice in the 1970s to help a person control certain physical and psychological responses. It uses electrical sensors to provide feedback on the body's reactions in a given situation. The feedback helps identify what adjustments to make. For example, a person might slow the rate of breathing to relieve anxiety or employ muscle relaxation to ease pain.

One goal of Spacelab-J was to train astronauts in biofeedback to overcome the unpleasant effects of motion sickness in space. During preparation for her flight, Jemison was coached on the method at NASA's Ames Research Center in Moffett Field, California. Both she and crewmate Davis, who served as the control, wore special wrist displays in flight. Jemison's display gave readings on her heart rate, blood pressure, and skin temperature, but Davis's screen was blank. Biofeedback worked for Jemison as a means of reducing motion sickness, but findings were not conclusive as to whether it would be effective for a larger sample of astronauts. In the years since Jemison's flight, biofeedback has been widely used by health-care providers as an alternative to medication.

EIGHT

SCIENCE AMBASSADOR

Traveling to space was both challenging and rewarding for Jemison, just as she always thought it would be. As a scientist, she was proud of the many experiments the crew conducted, but she did not envision continuing as an astronaut. Jemison knew there was no telling when she would be assigned to another mission, and besides, she was not "addicted to space."[1]

GOOD–BYE NASA

Ready to move on to her next adventure, Jemison resigned from NASA in 1993. NASA was surprised by her departure, and some insiders complained she was throwing away the valuable time and money the government had invested in her training. However, she was satisfied she had provided NASA and the

After spending a total of approximately 130 hours in space, Jemison resigned from NASA.

scientific community with consequential scientific research and had added much-needed diversity to the astronaut program. Jemison remained passionate about the importance of space travel and experimentation, but she felt she could be a better advocate for the space program outside of NASA.

Homer Hickam, Jemison's training manager for STS-47, admitted that NASA was not happy to see her leave. Nevertheless, he acknowledged Jemison's broader ambitions as a scientist. "I see Mae as sort of an all-around ambassador," he said. "She just really wanted to make a connection with the world."[2] Leaving her astronaut career behind allowed Jemison to pursue other interests and be a voice for science and space travel wherever she went.

MOVING ON

Following her time at NASA, Jemison sought a way to integrate social issues with technological advances. In 1993, she founded a technology consulting company in Houston called the Jemison Group that she still led as of 2017. In one of its first projects, the company designed and installed systems that generated solar thermal electricity in developing countries. She worked with Suncorp, a South African company, to develop a solar-energy system that could provide electricity not only when the sun was shining, but also during the night and at times of high demand. Another Jemison Group project provided satellite-based

SCIENCE
SPOTLIGHT

SATELLITES IN SPACE

One project undertaken by the Jemison Group was Alafiya, which means "good health" in the African Yoruba language. Project Alafiya was a satellite network designed to improve health-care delivery in remote parts of West Africa and other less developed areas. It relied on technology enabled by Syncom 2, NASA's 1963 satellite that was the first to be in sync with Earth's rotation period. In communications satellites, signals are sent by ground stations to the receiver antennas of satellites previously placed in space. The signals are then relayed back to Earth, enabling people in distant locations to access the transmitted information. Signals are differentiated by their wavelength and bandwidth. The greater the volume of information transmitted, such as data, images, and audio, the wider the bandwidth. Alafiya enabled health workers in developed countries to provide doctors and nurses in remote villages with the information they need to treat their patients.

telecommunications to deliver health information to remote communities in West Africa.

Jemison also founded BioSentient Corporation in 1999. BioSentient is a medical technology company that creates and sells equipment to monitor the body's vital signs. Users are trained to react positively during stressful situations. Jemison was able to apply her biofeedback research experience in developing this equipment.

From 1995 to 2002, Jemison was an environmental studies professor at Dartmouth College in Hanover, New Hampshire. One of the courses she taught was on space-age technology. To capitalize on Jemison's unique experience, the college created the Jemison Institute for Advancing Technology in Developing Countries. As director of the Jemison Institute, she helped coordinate projects based on technology to resolve or alleviate problems faced by developing countries, especially those on the African continent. The institute also served as a place to collaborate with other scientists through seminars and publications. The Jemison Institute organized a conference in 2000 called S.E.E.ing the Future (Science, Engineering and Education). The purpose of the conference, said Jemison, was "to shed light on the most effective use of government funding in science and engineering research."[3] It brought together scientists, artists, writers, businessmen, and theologians to

In addition to teaching college, Jemison worked to promote science to high school students and hospital patients.

discuss how science and engineering research affects society and how it should be encouraged. Said Jemison, "Science is investigated, engineering is advanced, technology developed and education offered based on the will of the public. That will relates directly to how well society and its leaders understand the pivotal role science and technology play in our everyday lives."[4]

Making Science Make Sense

In 1995, Jemison became chief ambassador for Bayer Corporation's award-winning program, Making Science Make Sense. This program, similar to much of Jemison's other work, seeks to promote science education across the United States through hands-on learning. The program works with Bayer employees, local organizations, and public schools to make science relevant for young and old alike. Jemison travels as Bayer's spokesperson to advance STEM (science, technology, engineering, and mathematics) education, science literacy, and diversity, and make science less intimidating and more accessible to the public.

BRIDGING ARTS AND SCIENCES

Jemison has remained committed to providing future generations with a strong science education. She, along with her siblings Ricky and Ada Sue, founded the Dorothy Jemison Foundation for Excellence (DJF) in 1994 in memory of their mother. This foundation develops and implements curriculum and innovative teaching methods. Jemison and her siblings made it the foundation's goal to help students grow into contributing members of society by achieving excellence in academics. The foundation places strong emphasis on teaching methods that rely on experiential learning, particularly in the field of science. DJF provides unique educational experiences for students, including its main initiative, an international science camp known as The Earth We Share (TEWS).

As part of her advocacy for science education, Jemison began giving lectures and interviews in the early 2000s to promote the blending of arts and sciences in education. She encourages people to see that science can be creative and art can be analytical. Jemison identifies both science and the arts as "avatars of human creativity," or ways in which humans attempt to influence and change the world.[5] According to Jemison, "Science provides an understanding of a universal experience, and art provides a universal understanding of a personal experience."[6] She asserts that science helps individuals understand the things that affect all humans, while art enables others to see how

The Earth We Share

As part of the Dorothy Jemison Foundation, Jemison started TEWS international science camp to promote science literacy. Students ages 12 to 16 attend the four-week summer camp, during which they analyze and propose solutions to current problems facing the world, such as how many people can be sustained globally with the resources we have. TEWS launched the Space Race Program in 2011 to train teachers and increase science understanding and success among underserved students in Los Angeles. Other TEWS efforts have included essay contests, online youth conferences, and international surveys.

the world's knowledge and understanding affect people at a personal level. Jemison emphasized the importance of both arts and sciences in her role as a professor-at-large at Cornell University from 1999 to 2005 and subsequently as an adjunct professor at Dartmouth's Geisel School of Medicine.

PROMOTING EQUALITY

Encouraging minorities to enter science fields has always been among Jemison's top priorities. When she was listed in *People* magazine's 1993 edition of the "50 Most Beautiful People in the World," she first saw her selection as "goofy," but then viewed it as an opportunity to broaden public perceptions about who can be a scientist. Said Jemison, "We need to change the image of who does science. That's important not only for folks who want to go into science, but for the folks who fund science."[7]

Leader-in-Residence

Jemison was selected as the Poling Chair of Business and Government at Indiana University's Kelley School of Business for the 2016–2017 academic year. She was the first African American to be chosen for this position. As a leader-in-residence, Jemison made periodic trips to the university to lecture and meet with students, fostering discussions about leadership, sustainability, and technology research and development. Jemison's goal for the year, as she described it, was to work with students on "understanding the vital connections between the physical and social sciences, as well as culture and art, [and] to problem solve and create robust solutions."[8]

In 2005, Jemison and two other US astronauts traveled to China to tour the Chinese space program.

Desegregating NASA

A program entitled "The Unlikely Story of NASA and the Civil Rights Movement: Race and the Space Race" aired on public radio in February 2010. Narrated by Jemison, it tells how NASA built its main research centers in Alabama, Texas, and Florida in the early 1960s, hiring numerous black engineers and test pilots. These early African-American scientists pushed for the desegregation of NASA's facilities in the South at a time when segregation was the norm. Jemison emphasized that the work done by those scientists built the foundation for current space-exploration technology.

Jemison has long advocated for more women and minorities to go into science, in part because they make up two-thirds of the US population but less than one-quarter of the workforce in science-related fields. She maintains women must be given a better chance to enter what are mostly male careers such as engineering. Her 2001 autobiography, *Find Where the Wind Goes,* chronicles her story as a young woman pursuing a science career. As a feminist and a voice for women of color across the globe, Jemison encourages women to be empowered first by believing in themselves and then by taking risks that will move them forward.

For her entire career, Jemison has been a role model for women wanting to work in science.

SHOOTING FOR THE STARS

T hroughout her life, Jemison has encouraged equality, fairness, and compassion in the way people treat each other. On a larger scale, she has encouraged the same in how nations interact with other nations. Jemison views space exploration as an ideal vehicle for productive collaboration. She maintains space exploration should not be a space race, as it was during the Cold War, but instead should involve cooperation with and inclusion of less-industrialized countries. Space exploration is a birthright of everyone on the planet, according to Jemison, who notes, "The most enduring benefits will come from exploration when the opportunity for participation encompasses everyone."[1] Her view is that all countries and

Jemison has become a powerful advocate for cutting-edge space exploration.

peoples should be involved in the study of space because everyone on the planet will have to share the cosmos.

WHY SPACE?

Ever since space travel became a reality, many have questioned its relevance to life on Earth. President Julius Nyerere of Tanzania once condemned Western countries for racing to reach the moon while African leaders were simply trying to reach their villages with education, modern medicine, and food. But Jemison, in her lifetime of advocacy for space exploration, has identified many ways in which advances made possible through the space program have aided humans in everyday life.

For example, artificial satellites of various kinds serve many useful purposes. Communication satellites launched into space enable radio and television transmission to the far reaches of the planet. Weather-tracking satellites warn of powerful storms, giving people a chance to prepare and protect themselves. The satellites of the global positioning system (GPS) are vital in helping people get from one location to another. Finally, sending humans into space has helped identify the range within which humans can adapt to different environmental conditions.

Jemison advocates for continuing space exploration because studying outer space has already produced so much worthwhile knowledge about the universe. She asserts that experiments conducted in space have fostered a better understanding of basic principles in physics, chemistry, and biology. The International Space Station affords an ongoing opportunity for making scientific advances in these fields. Space exploration, Jemison says, should encourage humans to "try to grasp, to understand, to know the secrets of the universe and . . . to belong."[2] As someone who viewed Earth from the vastness of space, she believes exploring space allows humans to develop an appropriate sense of their place in the universe.

The International Space Station, currently the size of a football field, carries on its cutting-edge research through the cooperation of five nations' space agencies.

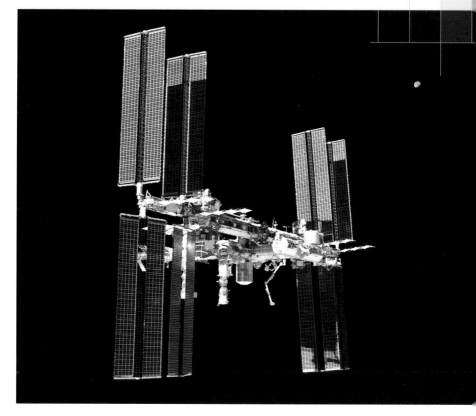

The International Space Station

The International Space Station (ISS), a permanent laboratory in Earth orbit, is the start of the global space collaboration Jemison envisions. Currently, it is the largest science and technology project of international scope and universal scale. Construction of the ISS has occurred in stages, beginning in 1998. The first component to be sent to space was the Russian cargo block, known as the *Zarya* module. Next, NASA launched *Endeavour*, the same shuttle Jemison flew on in 1992, to connect the *Unity* docking system to *Zarya*. This was the first step in the deployment of other shuttles that would attach to the ISS. In 2000, the Russian unit *Zvezda* was attached to provide living quarters and life-support systems for astronauts, preparing the way for the first crew to come aboard in October of the same year. The ISS has since been continually operated by a changing crew of between two and nine people, with six being the typical crew size in recent years. Crews have included astronauts from Canada, Europe, Japan, Russia, and the United States. These men and women work together on the ISS to test various technologies, do medical research, and develop innovative materials and processes that will enhance life on Earth. Construction of the ISS was completed in 2010. In 2016, it measured 356 feet (109 m) across and 290 feet (88 m) long, weighing approximately 940,000 pounds (430,000 kg).[3]

Jemison identifies three realms of space exploration. The first is the physical realm, which includes finding uncharted physical places, as when sailors struck out across Earth's oceans centuries ago. The second is the applied realm of exploration, through which human curiosity is called upon to solve a current issue in education, politics, society, technology, or other fields. The last is the imaginative realm of exploration, where people seek understanding about why things are a certain way and contemplate the possibility of creating something new. Jemison admits she favors the last realm, claiming, "The wonderful aspect of imaginative exploration is that many times [it] has yielded tremendous gains in the most unlikely, unexpected ways."[4]

Jemison believes space exploration taps into human curiosity and the desire to discover new frontiers.

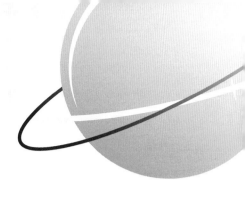

FUTURE
TECH

BONE GROWTH

During Jemison's STS-47 mission in space, she was a co-investigator in two bone cell research studies. Under normal conditions on Earth, bone health is significantly affected by physical activity. Weight-bearing activity in which muscles pull and push against bones causes new bone tissue to form. In contrast, insufficient activity, along with the aging process, can lead to bone loss and greater risk of falls and fractures. When humans travel in space, bones are not under the same stress as they are on Earth. One of Jemison's bone experiments in space looked at cartilage growth and bone formation in fertilized chicken eggs and rat bone cells. The other involved analyzing bone and muscle mass in crew members before and after the flight through magnetic resonance imaging.

Scientists know that wounds and fractures heal slowly in a microgravity environment because of the way blood circulates. Jemison is overseeing a long-term research project that concerns bone microencapsulation. Microencapsulation occurs when chemical substances, such as proteins, are surrounded by a coating. Researchers on this microencapsulation project are developing biomaterials made up of proteins and connective-tissue stem cells that could accelerate the healing process. In addition to benefiting space travelers, such materials could be useful to patients on Earth with nonhealing wounds, including burn victims and the elderly.

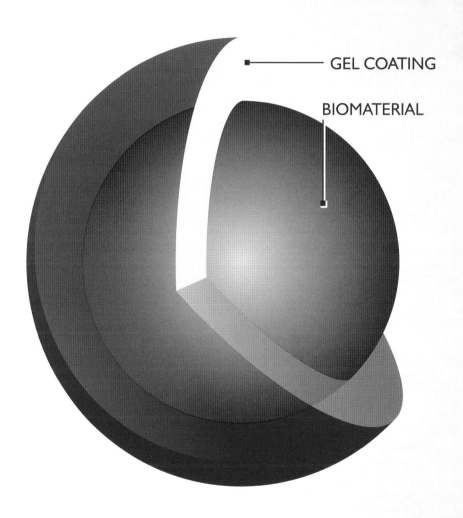

GEL COATING

BIOMATERIAL

Microencapsulation holds promise as a way of administering therapeutic biomaterials by encasing them in a gel coating that disintegrates over time.

TO THE STARS

Jemison's commitment to imaginative exploration led her to the most aspirational project of her life. In 2012, Jemison received a grant to undertake the 100 Year Starship project, a multidisciplinary effort that aims to make interstellar travel possible within the next century. Based in Houston, the project added an affiliate in Brussels, Belgium, in 2016, with plans to develop affiliates in Africa and Asia as well. With current technology, it would take 70,000 years of traveling for humans to reach Alpha Centauri, Earth's closest neighboring star system.[5] But Jemison and her team are determined to dramatically shorten the duration of the voyage and make such a journey happen within the next hundred years.

The most significant challenge in achieving this goal relates to energy. A trip of this distance would require much more powerful and enduring energy sources than the ones currently used to propel spacecraft. Technologies such as ion propulsion and nuclear fission or fusion hold some promise as massive energy generators. Jemison also acknowledges the need for creating effective life-support systems and sustainable habitats. Even with major leaps in technology, it would take years for an astronaut to travel to another star.

Jemison recognizes that sending humans to destinations within the solar system, such as Mars, will be the first major

100 Year Starship is a joint venture between NASA and the US Department of Defense. Jemison submitted the winning bid to launch the project.

step toward reaching another star system. Activities undertaken by 100 Year Starship have included conferences, lectures, essay contests, online forums, and the establishment of the Way Institute. The Way Institute is a research and development organization that aims to identify and advance the knowledge needed to facilitate interstellar travel. Since an essential component of planning for the future is cultivating future leaders, 100 Year Starship is invested in promoting STEM literacy and inspiring future generations of scientists. To that end, in 2013, Jemison published a series of children's books on the solar system to inspire young readers.

Jemison admits the concept of traveling to another star system may sound like fantasy. She notes people thought the same of classic science fiction writer H. G. Wells's story, published in 1901, about men landing on the moon. Yet less than 100 years later, men did indeed land on the moon. Today's advances in science and technology occur at a much faster rate than they did in Wells's time.

THE UNIVERSE, HER LABORATORY

Today, Jemison lives in Houston with her beloved cats. She travels and lectures extensively, speaking to young and old alike about social responsibility, empowerment, technology, and the discoveries that await humans through space exploration. Her inquisitive mind has allowed her to become an accomplished

SCIENCE
SPOTLIGHT

BREAKTHROUGH STARSHOT

Breakthrough Starshot, created by Russian entrepreneur Yuri Milner in 2016, is a research and engineering project aiming to invent spacecraft that can reach the Alpha Centauri star system by the next generation. Milner, along with English physicist Stephen Hawking, seeks to develop nanocrafts, which are tiny, robotic space vehicles that can travel 1,000 times faster than current spacecraft. The nanocrafts will consist of a tiny microelectric Starchip and a lightsail no more than several hundred atoms thick. The Starchip will be a tiny wafer containing cameras, a power supply, and navigation and communication equipment. Energy from the sun, collected on the surface of thin material stretched across the lightsail's frame, will propel the craft through space. Light beams will be used to power the nanocrafts through the solar system and beyond to Alpha Centauri, 25 trillion miles (40 trillion km) from Earth. Once the Starchip is able to be mass-produced, large numbers of nanocrafts can be sent into space to collect and transmit information. Jemison, who also promotes interstellar travel through her 100 Year Starship initiative, attended Breakthrough Starshot's introductory press conference in April 2016. She remarked, "Collectively we as humans are at a point in which, technologically, there's at least one feasible path to getting to another star within our generation."[6]

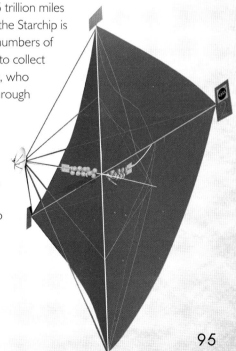

scientist and a visionary entrepreneur, all while inspiring others to dream big and aim high. In particular, she has been a role model for girls, young women, and people of color who might not otherwise have considered a career in science. As Jemison's closest college friend once observed, "She just had a different twist on life. If she saw it and she wanted to experience it, there was no barrier to her achieving it. She felt the world was her laboratory."[7] Through curiosity, determination, and hard work, Jemison accomplished her lifelong dream of space travel. With a limitless imagination that has enabled her to achieve great things, she is living proof that the sky truly is the limit!

Lego Space Heroes

A Lego set honors five NASA women who have been instrumental in the advancement of the space program. The five are computer scientist Margaret Hamilton, mathematician Katherine Johnson, physicist Sally Ride, astronomer Nancy Grace Roman, and physician Mae Jemison. The set includes a Lego-sized Hubble Space Telescope, a mini–space shuttle, and several Apollo-era instruments.

Jemison achieved her goal to travel in space, inspiring others to aim high and pursue their dreams.

TIMELINE

1956
Mae Carol Jemison is born on October 17 in Decatur, Alabama.

1960
The Jemison family moves to Chicago, Illinois.

1973
After graduation from Morgan Park High School in Chicago, Jemison begins college at Stanford University.

1977
Jemison graduates from Stanford with a bachelor of science in chemical engineering. She enrolls at Cornell University Medical College in New York City.

1979
Jemison works in Kenya for a summer with the African Medical Education and Research Foundation.

1981
Cornell University Medical College grants Jemison her doctor of medicine degree.

1983
Jemison begins serving with the Peace Corps as a medical officer in Sierra Leone and Liberia.

1985
Jemison applies to be a NASA astronaut.

1987
Jemison is accepted into NASA's astronaut program.

1988
During flight training, Jemison meets actress Nichelle Nichols, who played Jemison's favorite character on *Star Trek*.

1992
On September 12, as a crew member of the space shuttle *Endeavour*, Jemison becomes the first African-American woman to travel into space.

1993
Jemison resigns from NASA and forms the Jemison Group.

1994
The Jemison siblings establish the Dorothy Jemison Foundation for Excellence to promote educational innovation and science literacy.

1995
Jemison begins promoting science literacy for the Bayer Corporation and becomes a professor of environmental studies at Dartmouth College.

2001
Find Where the Wind Goes: Moments from My Life, Jemison's autobiography, is published.

2012
The 100 Year Starship project begins under Jemison's direction.

2016
Jemison becomes a leader-in-residence at Indiana University's Kelley School of Business.

ESSENTIAL
FACTS

DATE OF BIRTH
October 17, 1956

PLACE OF BIRTH
Decatur, Alabama

PARENTS
Charlie and Dorothy Jemison

EDUCATION
Morgan Park High School, Chicago, Illinois
Stanford University, Stanford, California (bachelor of science in chemical engineering)
Cornell University Medical College, New York, New York (doctor of medicine degree)

CAREER HIGHLIGHTS

- In 1983, Jemison was hired as Area Peace Corps Medical Officer for Sierra Leone and Liberia.

- On her return from Africa in 1985, Jemison worked as a primary care physician in Los Angeles, California.

- In June 1987, Jemison moved to Houston, Texas, and was in the first class of astronauts at Johnson Space Center following the space shuttle *Challenger* explosion.

- On September 12, 1992, Jemison was launched into space as a science mission specialist on the space shuttle *Endeavour*.

- Jemison resigned from NASA in 1993 and started several companies during the next few years.

- As a professor at Dartmouth College in Hanover, New Hampshire, from 1995 to 2002, Jemison lectured on the importance of increasing science literacy.

SOCIETAL CONTRIBUTIONS

- Jemison was the first African-American woman to travel into space.

- Using herself as a test subject, Jemison provided future space travelers with important information on adjusting their bodies to life in space.

- Jemison and her siblings started the Dorothy Jemison Foundation for Excellence to increase science literacy, particularly among underserved students across the United States.

- In 2012, Jemison initiated the 100 Year Starship project, a multidisciplinary research and development effort to make interstellar travel a reality within the next century.

CONFLICTS

- While at Stanford University, Jemison encountered a few professors who were skeptical of her abilities because of her age, race, and gender.

- Two weeks into her job with the Peace Corps, Jemison had to forcefully advocate for the medical evacuation of a critically ill patient, against the advice of US embassy staff.

- Jemison unexpectedly resigned from NASA in 1993 to pursue other scientific interests after completing only one mission in space.

QUOTE

"Science is investigated, engineering is advanced, technology developed and education offered based on the will of the public. That will relates directly to how well society and its leaders understand the pivotal role science and technology play in our everyday lives." –Mae Carol Jemison

GLOSSARY

adjunct
A low-ranking or temporary staff member.

artificial satellite
An unmanned spacecraft placed in orbit around Earth, the moon, or another planet to transmit information.

biochemistry
The branch of science concerned with the chemical processes that occur within living organisms.

biofeedback
Techniques used to monitor and control body reactions.

biomaterial
A material that is safe to use inside living tissue, especially as part of a medical device.

biomedical engineering
A branch of engineering dealing with the design of medical devices.

chemical engineering
A branch of engineering involving the use of chemistry in industry.

control
In a science experiment, the subject or group that does not receive treatment or testing and is used to measure how the treated or tested subjects compare.

cosmos
The complex and ordered system known as the universe.

hematology
The study of blood in health and disease.

interstellar
Occurring or situated between stars.

intravenous
Happening within or entering through a vein.

microgravity
Environment where the effects of gravity are minimized and objects appear to have little weight.

orbit
The curved path of a celestial object or spacecraft around a star, planet, or moon.

orbiter
The part of the space shuttle that carries the crew and payload into orbit around Earth.

residency
A training program for doctors after medical school, during which they become experts in their chosen specialty.

semiconductor
A solid material with unique properties related to how an electric current flows through it.

solar thermal
A system that uses energy from the sun to generate heat or electricity.

ADDITIONAL RESOURCES

SELECTED BIBLIOGRAPHY

Gubert, Betty K., Miriam Sawyer, and Caroline M. Fannin. *Distinguished African Americans in Aviation and Space Science*. Westport, CT: Oryx, 2002. Print.

Jemison, Mae. *Find Where the Wind Goes: Moments from My Life*. New York: Scholastic, 2001. Print.

Kevles, Bettyann Holtzmann. *Almost Heaven: The Story of Women in Space*. New York: Basic, 2003. Print.

Shayler, David, and Ian A. Moule. *Women in Space: Following Valentina*. Chichester, UK: Praxis, 2005. Print.

FURTHER READINGS

Gibson, Karen B. *Women in Space: 23 Stories of First Flights, Scientific Missions, and Gravity-Breaking Adventures*. Chicago: Chicago Review, 2014. Print.

Grayson, Robert. *Exploring Space*. Minneapolis, MN: Abdo, 2014. Print.

Jones, Tom. *Ask the Astronaut: A Galaxy of Astonishing Answers to Your Questions on Spaceflight*. Washington, DC: Smithsonian, 2016. Print.

Sparrow, Giles. *Spaceflight: The Complete Story from Sputnik to Apollo—and Beyond*. London: DK, 2009. Print.

WEBSITES

To learn more about Women in Science, visit **abdobooklinks.com**. These links are routinely monitored and updated to provide the most current information available.

FOR MORE INFORMATION

For more information on this subject, contact or visit the following organizations:

Kennedy Space Center Visitor Complex
State Route 405
Kennedy Space Center, FL 32899
866-737-5235
https://www.kennedyspacecenter.com/
The complex provides tours of the Kennedy Space Center and is home to the shuttle *Atlantis*. It also offers a shuttle-launch experience, a chance to see the earliest rockets, encounters with veteran astronauts, and 3-D space exploration shows.

National Space Society
P.O. Box 98106
Washington, DC 20090-8106
202-429-1600
http://www.nss.org/
The National Space Society is a grassroots organization that publishes an award-winning magazine on space travel and has a rich online library of books and videos on space.

Space Center Houston
1601 NASA Parkway
Houston, TX 77058
281-244-2100
http://spacecenter.org/
Owned by the nonprofit Manned Space Flight Education Foundation, Space Center Houston includes a museum with many artifacts from the space industry, including a 36-story Saturn V rocket and the room where NASA monitored the historic Apollo moon landing. Visitors may take a tram tour of the adjacent Johnson Space Center.

SOURCE NOTES

CHAPTER 1. ENDEAVOR TO DREAM

1. "STS-47 (50)." *Kennedy Space Center*. NASA, 29 June 2001. Web. 30 Nov. 2016.

2. Kenneth S. Thomas and Harold J. McMann. *U.S. Spacesuits*. New York: Springer Praxis, 2012. 372. *Google Book Search*. Web. 30 Nov. 2016.

3. Ibid.

4. Wayne Hale and Helen W. Lane. *Wings in Orbit: Scientific and Engineering Legacies of the Space Shuttle, 1971–2010*. Washington, DC: National Aeronautics and Space Administration, 2010. Print. 56.

5. Ibid.

6. Mae Jemison. *Find Where the Wind Goes: Moments from My Life*. New York: Scholastic, 2001. Print. 177.

7. Mae Jemison. "Executive Life: The Boss; 'What Was Space Like?'" *New York Times*. New York Times, 2 Feb. 2003. Web. 30 Nov. 2016.

CHAPTER 2. GROWING UP

None.

CHAPTER 3. TURBULENCE

1. "This Day in History, August 28, 1968: Protests at Democratic National Convention in Chicago." *History.com*. A & E Television Networks, n.d. Web. 30 Nov. 2016.

2. Mae Jemison. *Find Where the Wind Goes: Moments from My Life*. New York: Scholastic, 2001. Print. 62.

3. Deborah Kalb. *Guide to U.S. Elections*. Washington, DC: CQ, 2015. cxi. *Google Book Search*. Web. 30 Nov. 2016.

4. Ibid.

5. Mae Jemison. *Find Where the Wind Goes: Moments from My Life*. New York: Scholastic, 2001. Print. 114.

CHAPTER 4. CAREER DILEMMAS

1. Jesse Katz. "Shooting Star." *Stanford Today*. Stanford University, July/August 1996. Web. 30 Nov. 2016.

2. Mae C. Jemison. "Executive Life: The Boss; 'What Was Space Like?'" *New York Times*. New York Times, 2 Feb. 2003. Web. 30 Nov. 2016.

CHAPTER 5. DANCING DOCTOR

1. "Explore Our History." *Alvin Ailey American Dance Theater*. Alvin Ailey Dance Foundation, 2016. Web. 13 Oct. 2016.

CHAPTER 6. A HEART FOR AFRICA

1. "The Founding Moment." *Peace Corps*. Peace Corps, n.d. Web. 5 Oct. 2016.

2. Mae Jemison. "Executive Life: The Boss; 'What Was Space Like?'" *New York Times*. New York Times, 2 Feb. 2003. Web. 30 Nov. 2016.

3. "Schistosomiasis FAQs." *Centers for Disease Control and Prevention*. US Department of Health and Human Services, 7 Nov. 2012. Web. 30 Nov. 2016.

4. James Oberg. "7 Myths about the *Challenger* Shuttle Disaster." *Space on NBCnews.com*. NBCnews.com. 25 Jan. 2011. Web. 30 Nov. 2016.

NOTES CONTINUED

CHAPTER 7. THE NASA YEARS

1. Mae Jemison. *Find Where the Wind Goes: Moments from My Life.* New York: Scholastic, 2001. Print. 180.

2. "STS-47 (50)." *Kennedy Space Center.* NASA, 29 June 2001. Web. 30 Nov. 2016.

3. "STS-47 Mission Highlights Resource Tape." *YouTube.* NASA STI Program, 25 July 2011. Video. 59:19. Web. 30 Nov. 2016.

CHAPTER 8. SCIENCE AMBASSADOR

1. Bettyann Holtzmann Kevles. *Almost Heaven: The Story of Women in Space.* New York: Basic, 2003. Print. 132.

2. Jesse Katz. "Shooting Star." *Stanford Today.* Stanford University, July/August 1996. Web. 30 Nov. 2016.

3. "Dartmouth College Hosts National Science and Engineering Policy Think Tank." *Dartmouth News.* Dartmouth College, 10 Nov. 2000. Web. 30 Nov. 2016.

4. Ibid.

5. "Mae Jemison on Teaching Arts and Sciences Together." *YouTube.* TED Talks, 5 May 2009. Video. 8:02. Web. 30 Nov. 2016.

6. Ibid. 10:09.

7. Jesse Katz. "Shooting Star." *Stanford Today.* Stanford University, July/August 1996. Web. 30 Nov. 2016.

8. "Dr. Mae C. Jemison Named IU Kelley School of Business' Poling Chair of Business and Government." *DrMAE.com.* Dr. Mae Jemison, 20 Sept. 2016. Web. 30 Nov. 2016.

CHAPTER 9. SHOOTING FOR THE STARS

1. Mae C. Jemison. "Outer Space: The Worldly Frontier." *Sisterhood Is Forever: The Women's Anthology for a New Millennium*. Edited by Robin Morgan. New York: Washington Square, 2003. Print. 565.

2. Ibid. 566.

3. "Astronaut Candidate Program." *NASA*. NASA.gov, n.d. Web. 13 Oct. 2016.

4. Mae C. Jemison. "Outer Space: The Worldly Frontier." *Sisterhood Is Forever: The Women's Anthology for a New Millennium*. Edited by Robin Morgan. New York: Washington Square, 2003. Print. 564.

5. "Episode 43: Mae Jemison (100 Year Starship)." *YouTube*. The Energy Makers, 30 July 2012. Video. 6:54–8:00. Web. 30 Nov. 2016.

6. Amina Khan. "Starshot: Russian Billionaire and Stephen Hawking Want to Use Lasers to Send Tiny Spacecraft to Nearby Star." *Los Angeles Times*. Los Angeles Times, 12 Apr. 2016. Web. 30 Nov. 2016.

7. Jesse Katz. "Shooting Star." *Stanford Today*. Stanford University, July/August 1996. Web. 30 Nov. 2016.

INDEX

ABOUT THE
AUTHOR

Iemima Ploscariu is a historian who has published works varying from academic articles to faith-based devotionals. Originally from Romania, she now lives in California. She firmly believes in bridging the arts and sciences.